KU-477-819

Contents

What is your brain?

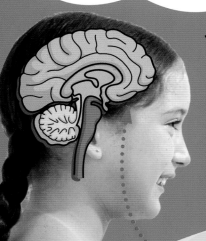

Your **brain** is inside your head. You think with your brain.

brain

It is always working.

Your brain is at
work even when
you sleep.

Your skull

Your brain is soft. Your **skull** keeps it safe. Your skull is made of two sets of bones.

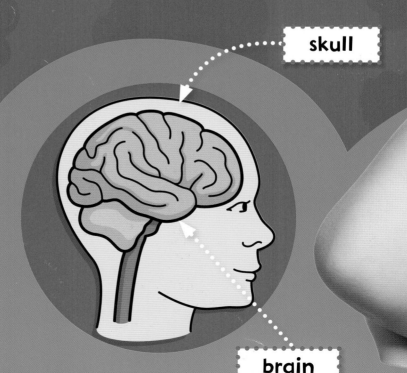

skull

brain

They make a kind of strong
box. Your brain is inside.

Nerves

Nerves carry messages
between your brain
and your body.

A long tube of nerves
runs down your back.
This is your **spinal cord**.

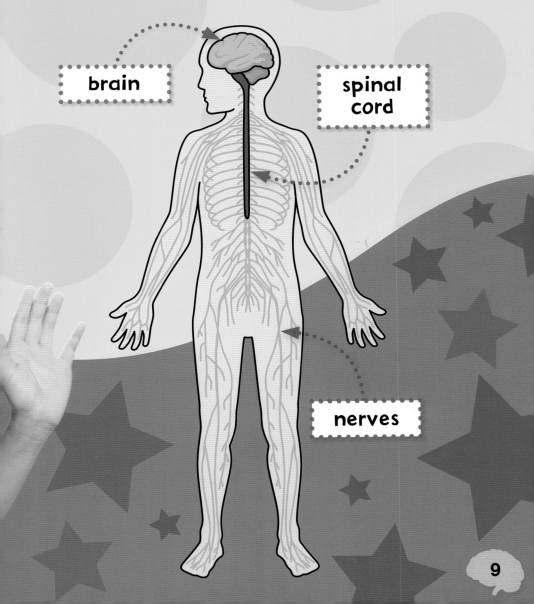

brain

spinal
cord

nerves

9

Reactions

Two kinds of messages are sent along your nerves. Your body tells your brain what it is doing.

Your brain tells your
body what to do.

Senses

You see something with your eyes. Nerves send that picture to your brain. Your brain tells you what you are seeing.

The same thing happens when you hear, taste, smell or feel something.

13

Quick as a flash

Some things you do without thinking.

You touch a hot cup.
You pull your hand back
fast. You do not think
about it. You just do it.

Memory

Your brain remembers things. It does this all by itself. You try a new food.

Your brain keeps track of how it tasted.

Your brain remembers
if you liked it or not.

A B C

Learning

You learn to ride a bike. Your brain remembers what your legs need to do. It remembers how riding a bike feels.

Your brain remembers better each time you practise. Before long, you can ride without thinking about it.

Feelings

Your feelings come from your brain. They can help you do the right thing at the right time.

You see a scary animal.
Your brain tells you to keep
away from it. You stay safe.

Healthy brain

Keep your brain healthy. Eat healthy foods. Eat lots of fruit, fish and vegetables.

Keep your brain busy.
Learn to do new things.
A busy brain is a
healthy brain!

23

Glossary

brain   the part of your body inside your head that controls your body, your thoughts and your feelings

nerves   thin strands in the body that send messages between the brain and the other parts of the body

skull   the bones in the head that protect the brain

spinal cord a thick bundle of nerves that starts at the brain and runs through the centre of the backbone